BIOGRAPHY OF THE BRIDE

The Divine Union between Christ and His Church

Amended edition with fresh insights

acg

Alice Claire Johnson

Alice Claire Johnson

ISBN 979-8-89043-668-9 (paperback)
ISBN 979-8-89130-464-2 (hardcover)
ISBN 979-8-89043-669-6 (digital)

Christian Faith Publishing
832 Park Avenue
Meadville, PA 16335
www.christianfaithpublishing.com

Printed in the United States of America

CONTENTS

Acknowledgments

I would like to say a special thanks to those who supported me in this holy adventure. You all have helped me put my thoughts and inspirations correctly on paper. I could not have done this without you.

To my husband, Terry Johnson, you gave me the gift of your grammar skills, editing, and especially your devotion.

To my children, Sunny, Joseph, and Amanda, for your constant support and encouragement, it is priceless.

To my local church family, for your prayers, love, and kindness, I wouldn't want to be without your friendships.

Most of all, to my Beloved Savior, Jesus Christ, for choosing the simple things of this life to confound the wise; Your loving-kindness stretches to the heavens.

All scripture is in the King James Version.

It's All About Her

acf

Song of the Bride

Lift up your eyes, toward the eastern sky
above the noise and the mire
The marriage chamber is prepared: hear the
thunder, see the lightning, feel the fire.
The angels exude hallelujahs, thousands
upon thousands join in song.
Awaiting "Behold the Bridegroom Cometh"
through the night so dark and long.
Her robe became white, in spite of battles and flood
Soon to be ready,
Drenched in His blood.
Biography of the bride, the true story of life,
United with her Groom: two become one, His eternal wife!

Introduction

One glorious Bride, with one mind and
one desire wholly for her Beloved.

—ACJ

Love shared between a man and woman finds its greatest fulfillment in wedded love. The courtship, wooing, and even the heartaches all contribute to *becoming one*, as declared in Genesis 2:24.

> Therefore, shall a man leave his father
> and mother, and cleave unto his wife;
> and they shall be one flesh.

This is a relationship of mutual submission of one to another, a beautiful reflection of Christ and His bride, the church. As we look into the life of the bride of Christ, we see the sacrifice of the Bridegroom King willingly giving His life for her while making a declaration of love.

In the very beginning, God said,

> It is not good that the man should be
> alone; I will make him an help meet for
> him. (Genesis 2:18)

Rather than getting right down to the making of Adam's helper, God created all the animals first (Genesis 2:19). Adam was brought into the classroom of God so he may see the need he had that only God could fulfill, a need Adam himself wasn't initially aware of. The creating of woman was absolutely essential to the plan of God and the continuation of humankind. It wasn't until Adam saw the animals paired did he realize his aloneness. Then and only then did God create Eve. They were perfectly suited for one another right from the very beginning. In every way, they were matched mentally, spiritually, emotionally, and physically—a picture of God's own design. Adam was lovesick over Eve to such an extreme he eventually put her before God.

> She took of the fruit thereof, and did eat,
> and gave also unto her husband with her,
> *and he did eat.* (Genesis 3:6)

All she did, without a word spoken, was hand him the fruit. Not hesitating for one minute, he did what she wanted and ate, disobeying God. Since then, man has been working hard to correct this by pulling away from woman and ruling over her, while the woman is still doing everything she can to attract the man and restore the garden love she once held and longed for. How mixed up things have gotten.

In Genesis 1:26–27, God said,

> Let us make man in our image, after our likeness; and let them have dominion over the fish of the sea, and the fowl of the air, and over the cattle, and over all the earth, and over every creeping thing that creepeth upon the earth. So God created man in His own image, in the

image of God created he him; male and
female created He them.

Equally yoked, both having dominion over the earth,
never ever was one to lord over the other.

Dr. Myles Monroe explained this concept beautifully:

> God took this spirit-man and He placed
> him in two physical forms; male and
> female. The spirit-man is neither male
> nor female.
>
> However, to fulfill His eternal pur-
> poses, God used two physical forms,
> called male and female, to express the
> one entity of man. Therefore, the essence
> of both male and female is the resident
> spirit within them, called man. In the
> Bible, when God speaks to humanity, He
> uses the term *man*. He doesn't address
> the male or female unless He's talking to
> individuals. Instead, He talks to the man
> within them both. (*Understanding the
> Purpose and Power of Women*)

Watchman Nee explained it this way:

> Eve was not created as a separate entity
> by a separate creation parallel to that of
> Adam. Adam slept, and Eve was created
> out of Adam. That is God's method with
> the church. God's "second Man" has
> awakened from his "sleep" and his church
> is created in him and of him, to draw her

life from him and to display the resurrection life. (*The Normal Christian Life*)

All attributes of the Triune God in man, both male and female, just as He is *one*, each giving honor to the other. This Triune God is three persons in one, each having their special place and task, never overstepping the other, and always in full agreement. God the Father is the invisible God and author of all. God the Son became flesh and is the brightness of God and the express image of His person (Hebrews 1:3). God the Holy Spirit is the indwelling God, the power and presence that dwells in mankind (Hebrews 6:19), the heart of God woven in perfect unity. This was the picture in the beginning. Our freedom in Christ takes us back to Genesis 2, where we are restored to the garden life in our hearts. The curse of Genesis 3 was forever removed by the second Adam at Calvary. We have been taken from death to life, complete in Him once again.

Judgment

I am my beloved's and his desire is toward me.

—Song of Solomon 7:10

When sin found its entrance, the intimate relationship between God and man was severed. At that moment, Adam and Eve suffered spiritual death and eventually physical death. Looking at the punishment for their disobedience, we will see that the curse of sin remains with each subsequent generation until it is wiped away through the Cross of Christ. He became our curse (Galatians 3:13) so we would not have to suffer eternal death.

> The Lord said to Satan, "Because thou hast done this, thou art cursed above all cattle, and above every beast of the field." (Genesis 3:14)

> And I will put enmity between thee and the woman, and between thy seed and her seed; It shall bruise thy head, and thou shalt bruise His heel. (Genesis 3:14–15)

To Eve, God said, "Your desire shall be for thy husband, and he shall rule over thee." (Genesis 3:16)

Finally to Adam God declared, "Because thou hast hearkened to the voice of thy wife, and hast eaten of the tree, of which I commanded thee, saying, Thou shalt not eat of it: cursed is the ground for thy sake; in sorrow shalt thou eat of it all the days of thy life." (Genesis 3:17)

When examining this portion of scripture in Genesis 3:16–19, God is speaking to the now-fallen man and woman. The *self-life* was born in the Garden that day because of mankind's disobedience to the command of God. Christ gave us power over this self-life through the Cross. We are given the first prophetic promise of hope in Genesis 3:15 where Christ would triumph over Satan (Genesis 3:15b). The woman's seed was to crush the devil's head, making all things subject to the authority of God. Scripture also reveals there will be enmity between the woman and the serpent (Genesis 3:14a). We see this more clearly as we peer into the pages of history and reflect on the abuse women have taken ever since the fall of mankind. Satan's disdain for her is obvious as she symbolized the church of God as a whole and became the avenue through which our Savior was born. Jesus brings reconciliation between God and man once again. This is the place where the power struggle between man and woman melts into oneness, back to their original state, reconciling them in the presence of God. The second Adam was so in love with His Eve (the church) that no price was too great to redeem her from the hands of the enemy.

2

The devastation of the fall in the Garden of Eden brought a cascade of false doctrines, beliefs, and practices. As the life of the bride unfolds before us, we will be delighted to discover the glorious life Christ has provided for us through His life, death, and resurrection. We will clearly see through scripture how the Holy Bridegroom held nothing back and freely gave, and still gives, His all. Jesus is coming back, not for a large host of little brides, but *one bride* with *one mind* and *one desire*—that of having the first commandment first place in our hearts. When we are able to grasp how His heart is ravished by even a glance from us, we will be filled with extravagant love for our Bridegroom King (Song of Solomon 4:9). As we begin to fix our gaze upon Him, we will become positively lovesick (Song of Solomon 2:5). Joy will flow in like a river when discovering the beauty and value the Bridegroom has for His bride. Learning more about her, we know more about ourselves and find a life of complete fulfillment in Christ.

> Let us be glad and rejoice and give Him glory, for the marriage of the Lamb has come, and His wife has made herself ready. (Revelation 19:7)

Marriage: One Man–One Woman

With the same intensity that the Father loves Jesus, He loves you.

—anonymous

What was God's design for marriage from the beginning? Did he not only take one rib from Adam for the creation of Eve? He said in Genesis 2:24,

> Therefore, a man shall leave his father and mother, be joined to his wife and they shall become one flesh.

God did not use the word *wives* here. So when did *wives* come into the picture? The very first to practice this was Lamech, an ancestor of Cain. Genesis 4:19 states,

> Lamech took unto him two wives.

This was just the beginning of a blatant violation of God's marital law of one man and one woman. For Lamech to keep his wives in this unheard-of relationship, he used great boasting, coupled with fear. He said in Genesis 4:23,

> Adah and Zillah, hear my voice; O wives of Lamech, listen to my speech! For I have killed a man for wounding me, even a young man for hurting me.

Lamech stated his name to declare his authority. He orchestrated a damaging use of religion to lead these women to gain ultimate control and then presented God as a seal of approval for his actions. "If Cain shall be avenged sevenfold, then Lamech, seventy-seven-fold." In other words, he was telling the two women if you leave or hurt me, not only will you face my wrath, but God will get you in the end as well. Fear was the knot that tied them together.

Jesus revealed the heart of God about marriage when He said,

> Wherefore they are no more twain, but one flesh. (Matthew 19:6)

No other than that relationship on earth can be more sacred. Our whole Christian life depends on our understanding of the marriage principle. If we fully comprehend and accept the natural law of marriage, we will have a very clear picture of the divine marriage. One man for one woman, no other combination will do. It is not only the design of God, but it is His own work that we are in Christ (John 15:1). Right from the beginning of time, before the foundation of the world, this Holy union was ordained: one bride for one husband (Genesis 1:27), the daughter of God for the son of God, given in marriage by the infinite Father, knit together by the Holy Spirit.

The more we give ourselves to Him, our Holy Bridegroom, the more He gives Himself to us. We find we can have as much or as little as we desire. He promises that if we draw near to Him, He will draw near to us (James 4:8). As our hearts are united by the bonding of the Holy Spirit, we are filled with the same love the Father has for the Son. This very love is how the Son loves us (John 15:9).

Prayer

Lord, show us that it is Your very own life You impart as we become one with You. Teach us what it means to abide. This most intimate act of obedience would make it impossible for us to, even for a minute seek a life apart from You. Deepen within us the sense of this Holy union. Reveal to us the revelation of this mystery and all the love and power it avails to us.

A Sinless Savior

Because the sinless Savior died, my sinful soul is counted free.
For God the just is satisfied to look on Him and pardon me.

—Charitie Lees Smith

Through a woman came the first sin, it was also a woman who birthed the Redeemer who washed sin away. In Matthew 1:20–21, it says,

> You shall call His name Jesus... He shall
> save his people from sin.

Jesus became the Holy sacrifice, sinless and perfect. How could Christ be born sinless since He had a mortal mother? In our human reproductive system, it is the man's seed that is a living organism; it fights for survival by swimming to the female seed/egg. It only knows it has to be the one to connect to ensure survival. It is through one live seed that sin is passed down from one generation to the next.

The Holy Spirit overshadowed Mary's (Luke 1:35) human egg containing the DNA of mankind, without the living seed of the male human. The result: a sinless birth, pure *Deity* in human form coming from the bosom of the Father to be from the "seed of a woman "(John 1:13). We stand back, dazed at such a gift, speechless to witness His profound humility as Deity willingly makes Himself a little lower than the angels (Hebrews 2:9).

He grew up before us a tender plant (Isaiah 53:2). At the age of twelve, He was clear of His purpose. He innately knew who His father was. Yet

> He was in this world, and the world was made by him, and the world knew him not. He came unto his own, and his own received him not. (John 1:10–11)

Scripture tells us He grew in wisdom and stature (Luke 2:52). He was the Word before the foundation of the world, became flesh, and dwelt among us (John 1:14).

> Jesus therefore knowing all things that would come upon Him. (John 18:4)

This reveals to us He knew exactly what Isaiah 53 said and the path that lay ahead for Him. The hardest thing for us to possibly understand is that He was "smitten by God" (Isaiah 53:4). Some believe Romans or Jewish leaders of that day were responsible for the crucifixion, but scripture clearly tells us it was God Himself who took full claim for this unimaginable event. He said,

> Yet it pleased the Lord to bruise Him; He hath put Him to grief. (Isaiah 53:10)

Before the fall in the Garden of Eden, both male and female shared mutual love and walked with God, scripture says "in the cool of the day" (Genesis 3:8), a divine fellowship.

When Eve succumbed to the craftiness of the devil, she became guilty of the first sin I call *unintentional,* the first

8

transgression. She then handed the forbidden fruit to her husband, Adam, standing right there beside her (Genesis 3:6). As he partook, just as his wife, he became guilty of the second sin, *intentional.* Both made up the whole of sin bringing forth death (James 1:15).

Mankind lost his status the moment he chose to rebel. In the Old Testament, God ordered the Israelites when in battle, to wipe out whole nations. It's hard to understand how a holy God could wipe out whole people groups, but when He looked at them, all He could see was sin. Other nations served false gods, usually made by their own hands, and did not believe in blood atonement for sin. From the time of Cain and Abel, mankind knew sin could only be covered by a blood sacrifice. These different people-tribes refused the God of Israel and His atonement requirements. Through the wickedness of his heart, Cain slew his brother, Abel. His jealousy and rebellion made Abel the first martyr for the blood sacrifice.

The shedding of the blood of sheep and goats did not please the heart of God (Hebrews 10:4–6). Though animals are sinless, their blood could only cover sins temporarily and could not give eternal life and complete forgiveness. The blood of animals had no atoning power; it could only act temporarily. Christ's blood, sinless in every way, brought eternal forgiveness, not just covering sin but, wiping it completely away (Colossians 2:13–15). We discover His blood not only destroys sin but heals and restores.

There were times in *my* walk with Jesus when it seemed I could not recover from heartache. It was too grave and deep. I prayed every day for the power to forgive and forget with no success. One day, I heard the soft, sweet voice of the Holy Spirit in the depth of my soul, "God is the only one who has the ability to forget, I programmed you to remember." Micah 7:19 says God will cast all our sins in the depth of the sea. Since the blood of Jesus is the only remedy for sin, may I take liberty and say this sea is made up of our Savior's blood established before time and eternity?

When the pain returns to my mind repeatedly, I do not become discouraged by my own weakness as I've come to know I have the ability through Christ to forgive when it begins to subside with each passing day. For some the process may be quick, and for others take a lifetime.

> For when I am weak, then am I strong. (2 Corinthians 12:10)

> The seat of the memory is the heart. (A. W. Pink)

> We were programmed to remember for the simple purpose to never forget Him. (ACJ)

Jesus Had a Stepfather

A beautiful example of a love relationship between the heavenly Father and His Son is illustrated in Joseph, the husband of Mary, the stepfather of Jesus. In an ancient Hebrew marriage, a contract would be signed long before the couple ever comes together. Very often it was an agreement between both parents of the prospective bride and groom. The contract was specific about the time, place, and groom. They were literally married at the signing of this agreement although not consummated at that time.

When reading Matthew 1:18–19, the scripture states,

> When His mother Mary was espoused
> to Joseph before they came together, she
> was found with child of the Holy Ghost.

A pregnancy outside the guidelines of the Law would mean public humiliation and possibly death to the woman. This was more than a threat; it was the requirement of the Law.

What we learn about Joseph through scripture is of his righteousness before God (Matthew 1:19a). His compassion toward Mary was evident by his decision to protect her from public disgrace and death by giving her a bill of divorcement, quietly sending her away (Matthew 1:19b). Joseph was initially fearful as he knew by the law what was required of him.

An angel of the Lord came to him and stated, "fear not to take unto thee thy wife." (Matthew 1:20)

He compassionately chose to protect Mary even when he knew the baby she carried wasn't his. We can be sure he was a man of prayer and sensitive to the voice of God. Four times, that we know of, through Joseph's life, he received warnings and instructions through dreams (Matthew 1:20; 2:12, 13, 19, and 22). The relationship between heaven and earth in the heart of Joseph through his prayers had already been long established. God the Father entrusted him with the life and care of His own very vulnerable infant Son and the woman who bore Him. It has never been recorded that Joseph resented or mistreated the little boy he would raise as his own. This was highly unusual.

We know both Joseph and Mary suffered persecution. The stigma of a pregnancy outside the boundary of the Law brought disdain from the community as we see when the couple traveled to Bethlehem to be counted in a mandatory census (Luke 2:1–7). Moments prior to the birth of her child, the innkeeper sent them to a dirty and cold stable. Johnathan Edwards eloquently describes the scene.

> The inn was taken up by others, that were looked upon as persons of greater account. The Blessed Virgin, being poor and despised, was turned or shut out. Though she was in such necessitous circumstances, yet those counted themselves her better would not give place to her. (*The Excellency of Christ*)

The infant of God was born in a barn, surrounded by humility, wrapped in swaddling, held by His mother, and protected by a loving stepfather.

Hidden to the ongoing census throng outside, prophecy of His birth was fulfilled that day. This special couple remained loyal to the will of God despite the malicious gossip and rejection they endured.

A point that may be pondered is the mirroring of His mother's features. Could it possibly be with only one set of human chromosomes this little boy was born amazingly resembling the female who gave Him birth? It would be just like God to include the whole of man even in the birth of His only Begotten Son.

Coming from my own experience, my three beautiful children were also blessed with a stepfather. There has never been a thought of a blood connection; this is not what makes him so loved by them. Just as Joseph lovingly cared for and watched over his family, this stepfather is a man pleasing the heart of God. One Father's Day, I wrote this poem for him:

Never a man finer than he
A father of two and also of three.
Acts like his mother, at times is a hoot, but,
most like his father, deep is the root.
No greater example of a father is true, my
love, my life, my beautiful you!

The Beauty of Humility

God bestows His blessings without discrimination.
The followers of Jesus are children of God and they
should manifest the family likeness by doing good
to all, even those who deserve the opposite.

—F. F. Bruce

Jesus's example of washing His disciple's feet perfectly modeled the greatest humility. Only the poorest and lowliest of servants in the ancient community washed the feet of others. Jesus shocked all those around Him, as evidenced by Peter's exclamation:

> Thou shalt never wash my feet! (John 13:8a)

To Peter's surprise, Jesus answered,

> If I wash thee not, thou hast no part with me. (John 13:8b)

Jesus painted such a vivid picture in the minds of His disciples that it still marks us to this day. Without the full cleansing work of redemption at the moment of salvation, the disciples could not have any place with Him.

Jesus stated, "He that is washed needeth not save to wash his feet, but is clean
every whit." (John 13:10)

We are completely cleansed when we are born again,
and this need not be repeated. Repentance, renewal, restoration, and growth are ways we experience continual cleansing, ultimately contributing to an abiding heart. This valuable parable also teaches another lesson on humility. The
greatest among us is to be the servant of all (Luke 22:26).
The example Jesus demonstrated for us in the washing of
feet showed us how to humble ourselves before our beloved
brothers and sisters, honoring them, and wiping away selfish
pride.

In John 13:18, Jesus explained there would be one of
His own who would betray Him.

He that eateth bread with me hath lifted
up his heel against me.

What fitting language to express betrayal since He had
just finished washing the feet of His disciples *including* Judas.
Every opportunity was given to Judas to change his mind.

Jesus said, "Most assuredly I say unto
you, one of you will betray me." (John
13:21)

Judas at this point realized Jesus knew of his intentions
but still chose to rebel. When sitting at the table, Jesus dipped
His bread into the bowl and handed it to Judas signifying a
close personal friendship. It was Judas who chose betrayal.
After receiving the bread from Jesus, the bread of life, he gave
himself over to Satan. Judas himself chose death over life.

Very few were aware of what was happening around the table that night. No one questioned Judas's abrupt departure; he would not have been suspected of anything out of the ordinary. He was their valued and trusted treasurer. It was Jewish tradition to purchase the necessary Passover items for the poor so all would be able to participate in the celebration.

It couldn't have been more natural for Judas to be the one to leave at that moment, so he could represent the disciples' group.

Scripture informs us that "it was night" (John 13:30). This is significant information because it implies more than the evening hour. We have come to understand the *darkness of the hour* was upon them. There was a traitor in the group who had rejected Christ and had given Satan free access.

> "Hail, Master!" exclaims the traitor. These words are like two poisonous daggers in the heart of the Holy One. He calmly accepts them, nor does He refuse even the infernal kiss itself. (F. W. Krummacher, *The Suffering Saviour*)

The idea of crucifixion and death never entered the mind of Judas; he thought the choice made to betray his Rabboni was harmless.

> And he that betrayed him had given them a token, saying whomsoever I shall kiss that same is he; take him, and lead him away safely. (Mark 14:44)

It wasn't long before he could see how very deceived he had been and could not live with his own decision (Matthew 27:5).

> After Jesus received Judas' kiss of betrayal, He stepped forward and asked the crowd of militia, "Whom seek ye? They answered him, Jesus of Nazareth. Jesus said unto them, I am he…" As soon then as he had said unto them, "I am He," *they went backwards, and fell to the ground.* (John 18:4–6)

The words *went backward* come from the Greek word *aperchomai*. In this case, the words depict the soldiers and temple police *staggering* and *stumbling backward*, as if some force has hit them pushing them backward. The word *fell* is a Greek word *pipto*, which means to *fall*. It was used to depict *a person who fell* so hard, it appeared that he *fell dead* or *fell like a corpse*. And again, it was so beautifully stated in this article:

> When the Great "I Am" opens His mouth and speaks, every power that attempts to defy Him or His Word is pushed backward and shaken until it staggers, stumbles, and falls to the ground! (Rick Renner, *Roman Soldiers Knocked Flat by the Power of God*)

What kind of choices are we making? If we are to walk in true humility, we must make the same kind of choices Jesus made while walking out His life here on earth. He emptied Himself by taking on the form of a servant (Philippians 2:7). We must do the same if you want to be great in God's kingdom you must be the servant of all (Matthew 23:11). He was obedient by choice in every area of His life even unto death (Philippians 2:8). We are to take up our cross, too, and follow Him (Luke 9:23). He was, and is, to come, the beauty of true humility embodied in human form (Colossians 2:9). Amid heaven arrayed in all meekness and gentleness, He remains forever the Lamb of God, the Great I Am, our humble Bridegroom King.

> A kiss can seal or a kiss can betray,
> To wit: Judas' kiss of betrayal. (ACJ)

No Price Was Too Great

The Cross and the
Passover Lamb

God gives us the cross, and then the cross gives us God.

—Jeanne Marie Guyon

When discussing the Passover Lamb, no other animal could have depicted Jesus more appropriately. The lamb is naturally harmless, gentle, and innocent. When studying Exodus chapter 12, we learn the sacrificial lamb must be without blemish. The slightest imperfection and it would have been rejected by the priest. Examining the life of Christ, God's lamb, we see an unblemished, holy life. He was in all points tempted as we are, but without sin (Hebrews 4:15), a pure conception, begotten by the Holy Spirit, born of a virgin, "in him is no sin" (1 John 3:5). The lamb, in the prime of His manhood, exists as the lamb of the first year as the Law required. In Exodus 12:3–6, the command was to separate the lamb from the rest of the flock for a total of four days. It had to be placed under close scrutiny to insure a spotless sacrifice.

When reflecting on this fact, it is incredible to observe the similarities between Christ's last days before and during crucifixion and the lamb in Exodus.

He rode on a donkey through the streets of Jerusalem proclaimed as king in triumphant entry, completely set apart and distinct from all mankind. Jesus officially presented Himself as the *Messiah King* (John 12:14). As we look in the synoptic gospels, we see one remarkable event after another during the last week of the Messiah's life, the bleating lamb, chosen one of God, slain before the foundation of the world (Revelation 13:8), now separated out, scrutinized by Pharisees, Sadducees, soldiers, commoners, and everyone in between.

> Never man spake like this man. (John 7:46)

Even Pilate declared three times, "I find no fault in him" (John 18:38, 19:4, 19:6). He is the Lamb without spot or wrinkle, one of God's own choosing.

There would be no bridal story without the Blood of the Passover Lamb. Jesus willingly said, "Yes," to the cross and the sacrifice of His very own life for the redemption of mankind. He stated

> No man takes it from me, but I lay it down myself. I have power to lay it down, and I have the power to take it up again. This commandment I have received of my Father. (John 10:18)

In nursing school, we had the opportunity to learn what people may experience when under tremendous stress. In the Garden of Gethsemane, we see the Lamb of God in deep anguish with sweat like great drops of blood (Luke 22:44), a rare and very dangerous phenomenon called *hematidrosis*. In this condition, subcutaneous capillaries engorge and then burst because of enormous pressure forcing blood and sweat through the skin pores. Jesus said His soul was exceedingly

21

sorrowful even unto death (Matthew 26:38). He began to shed His holy blood right there in the Garden, saying yes to the will of God:

> Nevertheless not My will, but Yours be
> done. (Luke 22:42)

The water and blood are always flowing together, never one without the other, the blood and the spirit, a perpetual stream flowing with the purpose to take away sin, conquering death, and redeeming His bride. That same blood flowed not because of a bloodthirsty, sadistic mob. They became angrier and angrier because God's chosen Lamb supernaturally did not pass out because of their brutality. He willingly chose to lay down His life:

> Greater love hath no man than this, that
> a man lay down his life for his friends.
> (John 15:13)

A crown of thorns ruthlessly pierced the Savior's brow so mankind can wear a crown of righteousness laid up for Him (2 Timothy 4:8). Blood-soaked hair and beard as the redeeming blood gushed down His cheeks.

The thorns and thistles that hedge itself around our minds by the enemy of our souls lost all power that day as it was covered in blood, His holy blood. No longer can addictions and fear keep us bound when we are bathed in this blood. Fixing our thoughts on Him produces a sound mind (2 Timothy 1:7). The curse the earth received because of man's disobedience (Genesis 3:17–18) was now being paid for as well, for He wore the curse of the thorns on His own brow. All heaven and earth are redeemed by the holy blood of the perfect sacrifice. According to F. W. Krummacher,

Ah, see! His bleeding arms are extended wide; He stretches them out to every sinner. His hands point to the east and west; for He shall gather His children from the ends of the earth. The top of the cross is directed toward the sky; far above the world will its effects extend. Its foot fixed in the earth; the cross becomes a wonderous tree, from which we reap the fruit of an eternal reconciliation. (*The Suffering Saviour*)

Not one bone was broken, fulfilling Psalm 34:20 (see Exodus 12:46 and Numbers 9:12). He was roasted in the furnace of affliction. He died, having His hands and feet pierced, just as an animal over an open fire, always and forever satisfying the heart of God, paying the penalty for the remission of sin. It usually took a man a day or two to die in this manner, but because of the brutal beating He received, it only took six hours. The greatest demonstration of His love for His church, *His beloved bride*, was during the last four days of His life. The Lamb of God who takes away the sins of the world (John 1:29), it was His blood that was poured out on the altar of the cross and covered the ground below. In Jewish tradition, the high priest poured the blood over the holy altar of God; this we've come to know is a representation of the blood poured out at the foot of the wooden cross in a temple called Calvary. He now has changed the earthly temple to one made without hands.

Behold all things are become new. (2 Corinthians 5:17)

One drop of Christ's blood is worth more than heaven and earth. (Martin Luther)

The Blood Speaks

The Blood has a voice, and it's calling you to the throne of grace.

—Lance Wallnau, "God's Word to You in 2022," YouTube

On my journey to become a registered nurse, it was necessary to identify the components and purposes of our human blood as part of the curriculum. This blood contains four main parts: red cells, white cells, and platelets suspended in plasma. Each part has its own specific function. When we have a greater understanding of the natural, the supernatural will be easier to grasp and apply to our own everyday lives. I will first discuss *in basic form*, the natural function of our blood, its duties and the importance of each.

- *Red blood cells*, also called hemoglobin, are made in our bone marrow. These cells are continually picking up oxygen each time we inhale and deliver air to the lungs. With blood passage throughout the entire body and returning to the lungs, these hardworking little cells exchange oxygen with carbon dioxide (waste product) to be exhaled.
- *White blood cells*: these cells are critical as a part of the body's immune response system. I consider them a kind of infantry engaged in battle, fighting infection and disease. These little soldiers ingest

foreign agents and debris by producing destructive antibodies.

- *Platelets*, also known as thrombocytes, are fascinating little cells that are able to come together to form clots when damage has occurred. They partner with white blood cells to fight infection and together quickly begin the healing process.
- *Blood plasma* is the liquid portion of our blood that is necessary to carry the blood components, nutrients, proteins, and hormones to all parts of the body. Removal of waste products through our amazing circulatory system is then complete.

Although the definitions here are simplistic and by no means comprehensive, the miracle of the blood is undeniable. Looking directly at our blood, we can see how the life of the body is in the blood. It nourishes, hydrates, cleanses, and works to maintain homeostasis (balance). It is no coincidence this natural process mirrors that of the greater supernatural Blood of Jesus.

Our circulatory system contains an amazing natural miracle... *This blood has a voice!* In Genesis 4:10, we read God speaking to Cain concerning his brother Abel:

> And he said, what hast thou done? The voice of thy brother's blood crieth unto me from the ground.

Even after Abel was dead, his blood was crying out to God for vengeance. Although our blood speaks, it does not consider religion or ethnicity. Incredibly, blood simply carries the very essence of life and speaks one universal language.

Our insight into the blood will help us grasp the infinite power of the Blood of Jesus Christ.

Back to the Beginning

When God formed Adam, He breathed into his nostrils (Genesis 2:7) transferring His own breath into Adam's lungs. As the lungs received this life-giving breath, Adam inhaled the very *essence of God.* It was not yet complete! From the first inhalation, this holy wind filled each red blood cell with life-giving oxygen. The body became fully alive with living blood that spoke!

There is no life apart from the blood. As we discussed in an earlier chapter, the relationship between Adam and Eve had changed because of their sin and subsequent spiritual death. We can be comforted by Jesus's sinless life, death, and resurrection bringing complete restoration to man once again. Therefore, a new and living way has been made. Death was swallowed up in victory (1 Corinthians 15:54). He took our place, tore down every barrier, and now stood as our Redeemer. His life-giving blood speaks a better word than that of Abel (Hebrews 12:24). Jesus speaks peace, mercy, love, healing, and forgiveness. We are now covered in the living blood of our Savior. When God looks at us, He sees His Son as we are now one with Him.

With the revelation of this life-filled blood, we can know intimately the meaning of Ephesians 4:4–7:

> There is one body, and one Spirit, even as
> ye are called in one hope of your calling,

one Lord, one faith, one baptism. One
God and father of all, who is above all,
and in you all.

We are one family, one blood, the human
family, "And hath made of one blood all
nations of man." (Acts 17:26)

The bride filled with the presence of God flowing
through her veins has now put on the new man created in
righteousness and true holiness (Ephesians 4:24).

Therefore if any man be in Christ, he
is a new creature: old things are passed
away; behold all things are become new.
(2 Corinthians 5:17)

The closer we draw to Him the more His nature is man-
ifested and revealed in us (Acts 4:13). His shed blood covered the mercy seat of heaven and the perfection of His life
redeemed ours (Hebrews 9:12 and Colossians 1:20). When
we need healing, all the components of His blood supernaturally work on our behalf. He took on our sin, sickness,
and sorrow by the crushing of Calvary; willingly He shed
his blood for mankind. The parallels between blood's natural
and supernatural healing capabilities will help us understand
the wholeness that is ours to receive.

The Darkness

*He it is who was crucified with the sun and moon
as witnesses; and by His death salvation has come to
all men, and all creation has been redeemed.*

—Saint Athanasius of Alexandria

The Lamb's own body, the Firstfruit of God (1 Corinthians 15:23), was now crushed under the pressure of the hand of the Father; Jesus willingly submitted Himself to the discipline of God. The darkness could be nothing less than supernatural following the light of midday. We should logically rule out an eclipse since this phenomenon is a relatively brief period where the grave darkness experienced at the time of the cross lasted three hours. All of heaven hushed during this most solemn time. The Light was removed from the sun as sin now lay heavily on the Sun of Righteousness (Malachi 4:2).

> In that day, declares the Sovereign Lord,
> I will make the sun go down at noon
> and darken the earth in broad daylight.
> (Amos 8:9)

It appeared for the first time in all eternity, *darkness* had overcome *light*. As difficult as it is to understand, this darkness was a mysterious shield to all God's children, as we were spared the most gruesome details.

I once believed God the Father had turned His face from His only Begotten Son on the cross because the world's sin was placed on Him. In my early reasoning, the darkness that swept over the earth and the massive quake that followed was proof. It wasn't until I began to understand "God is One," who can never be anything other; God the Father, God the Son, God the Holy Spirit. My new perspective was solidified by Colossians 2:9:

> For in him dweleth all the fullness of the Godhead bodily.

The sun and the earth were indeed witnesses but not of the rejection of the Father. On the contrary, Athanasius, an early Christian, stated,

> The sun veiled His face, the earth quaked, the mountains were rent asunder and all men were struck with awe. These things showed the Christ on the cross was God and that all creation was His slave and was bearing witness by its fear to the presence of its master. (*Incarnation*)

In no way did God the Father withdraw His love.

> This is My beloved Son, in whom I am well pleased. (Luke 3:22)

He was God's Beloved throughout all time and eternity. God's love never ceases (1 Corinthians 13:8).

> At the stroke of three, when the sacrifices were to begin in the Jewish temple, Jesus Christ thundered, "It is finished." (John 19:30)

> He shall see the travail of His soul, and be satisfied. (Isaiah 53:11)

> He poured His soul out unto death. (Isaiah 53:12)

When some heard His cry, they couldn't comprehend; they thought He called out to Elijah (Matthew 27:47). Yet nowhere in history is recorded a declaration filled with more relief than this. It was a job well done, nothing left out, perfect and complete.

As I read the book *Jesus and the Undoing of Adam* by C. Baxter Kruger on this moment in history, I felt his statement said it far more clearly than I did.

> In the greatest of ironies, the cry of Jesus, "My God, My God, why have You forsaken me?" actually sets in motion a line of thought that completely reinterprets what is happening on the cross. Far from being a perverse moment when the angry God pours His wrath out upon the Son and utterly rejects him, the cross is the moment when the Father absolutely refuses to forsake His Son, the moment of moments when He does not hide His face, or turn His back upon him in disgust. Here according to the Psalm and its interpretation of the event, there is no

forsaking at all. In fact, the Psalm tells us that the coming generations will see this event not as divine rejection, but precisely as divine presence and rescue and salvation. (p. 61)

In the ninth hour, out of utter darkness Jesus cried out "My God, My God why have you forsaken Me?" (Matthew 27:46)

It was here where Jesus pointed to Psalm 22, telling them the story as it unfolded before their eyes. This declaration stated not once but twice, quoting word for word the holy scriptures they all knew so well. No doubt this must have shaken the religious leaders standing by to their very core. They now knew Jesus truly was the Son of God. Although His body was in the very shadow of death, His mind never was. No price too great to set His bride free. She was always on His mind.

Have you ever been in a place where you wondered where God went? I remember a time I was so brokenhearted all I could do was breathe, and if that wasn't *on autopilot*, I wouldn't have had the strength to do that. I was walking in the shadow of death yet not forsaken. In that moment when I despaired even of life, I reached over and opened my Bible. The scripture unfolded before my eyes, as if a divine hand turned the pages to say,

I am nigh to the broken hearted and to those of a contrite spirit. (Psalm 34:18)

I was not alone. There in the deepest sorrow, He stretched out His arms and embraced me, and I, by faith, embraced Him back. Instantly, comfort filled my soul, and I knew I could go on living. God's word gave me hope and a new measure of peace I didn't have just seconds before.

Our Lord's love for the written word was obvious in life and now in death on a tortured cross. He never argues His case before God by questioning Him, but on the contrary, He was pointing to Psalm as His human body was being crushed as grapes from of the vine and then poured out as wine on the altar of the cross. It was in this darkest hour the Man of Sorrows revealed justice. Even though it was the darkest hour for Jesus, we can't think for one moment God was displeased with Him. It was God's plan to bruise Him (Isaiah 53:10) and to lay the weight of the world's sin upon the shoulders of the Righteous One, the Sinless One, the Holy and Blameless One, the Lamb of God's own choosing (Matthew 12:18). Jesus nevermore lovely than when being obedient to His death. Remember, whole nations were destroyed because of sin. Jesus bore the sins of the world past, present, and future. He stood in our place willingly taking man's rejection and judgment to the very end of His life. The "Why" (Mark 15:34) He cried was for us (Isaiah 42:1–4). His resolve and total submission were evident in His statement, "It is finished" (John 19:30a). Perfect obedience was exhibited to the end (Philippians 2:8). He humbly bowed His head in death (John 19:30b).

The first Adam felt the sting of separation by spiritual death because of sin. The second Adam understood and bore that separation in His own body, reconciling us back into the family of God. The Father personally taught our first earthly parents about the shedding of blood; they in turn taught their sons (Genesis 4:4). He, too, was the very first to shed blood because of sin and was the first to make a covering for man's nakedness (Genesis 3:21).

The Captain of our Salvation was made perfect through suffering. His spotless soul bore our grief and took our punishment, all for us, His beloved bride. He closed His eyes in death. He was given a respectable burial by tender loving hands. The tomb chosen was the absolute best because He suffered the most, He suffered enough. The best the world could offer was a borrowed tomb of a rich man. The Son of Man had nowhere to lay His head, even in death. He descended into the bowels of the earth for three days to loosen the chains of death and the grave (Ephesians 4:9). Light overcame darkness through the power of His blood (1 Corinthians 15:54).

I love the beautiful wording written by F. W. Krummacher:

> The Lord withdrew Himself from the eyes of men behind the black curtain of appalling night, as behind the thick veil of the temple. He hung there full three hours on the cross, His thorn-crowned head drooping on His breast, involved in that darkness. He is in the Most Holy Place. He stands at the altar of the Lord, He performs His sacrificial functions. He is the true Aaron, and at the same time the Lamb. (*The Suffering Saviour*)

The Lamb of God was now carrying His own blood across the threshold of the Holy of Holies to cover the mercy seat while renting the dividing curtain in two (Mark 15:38). This curtain represented His own flesh (Hebrews 10:20). He had a threefold purpose in mind: first to appease the wrath of God against sin, second to bring many to salvation (Romans 5:19), and lastly to make a way for all to enter into the Holy of holies, no longer a middle wall of partition between Jews and Gentiles from His glorious presence (Ephesians 2:14).

By the blood of this spotless Lamb, the old covenant with all its rituals and ordinances came to an end, and a new one took its place. His bride's debt is now *paid in full* by her Redeemer, her Husband, and her Passover Lamb who is seated at the right hand of God (Acts 7:56). His beloved was brought out of darkness into His glorious light (1 Peter 2:9).

It Was Always For Her

acj

36

His Death

Who delivered up Jesus to die? Not Judas, for money; not Pilate, for fear; not the Jews, for envy; but the Father, for love!

—Octavius Winslow

We need to carefully examine some of the most significant events surrounding the death of Jesus, especially the last sequential moments. The soldiers were commanded by their leader to insure the three men on the crosses were truly dead. When the soldiers arrived on the scene, they observed two of the prisoners on either side of Jesus were still alive. The soldiers agreed to break their legs to facilitate a quick and merciful death. This kind of physical trauma causes the body to enter a neurogenic shock state brought on by severe pain drastically affecting the nervous system. Heart failure inevitably soon follows. It doesn't sound very merciful to us looking on, but these men could have hung there for hours if left to nature and the elements.

When the soldiers came to Jesus, they could see He was already dead and decided not to break His legs, fulfilling the prophecy:

> Not one bone shall be broken. (Psalm 34:20)

But to be absolutely certain of death, one of the soldiers drew his sword and thrust it into the side of the Lamb of God piercing the myocardial sack of His heart. We can be reasonably sure Jesus was dead at this point as His blood had already begun to coagulate. The blood plasma had separated from the blood serum in His heart, as we read,

> And forthwith came there out blood and
> water. (John 19:34)

The Greek translation declares it was like a shower. This is He who came by blood and water, Jesus Christ, not only by water, but water and blood. It is the Spirit who bears witness because the Spirit is truth (1 John 5:6). As with the birth of a newborn baby comes by water and blood, so did He as the first born of many brethren (Romans 8:29).

This caused the final last drop of His holy blood to pour out like a drink offering on a wooden altar that day. He gave up His spirit and just that quick the last of His life's blood poured forth. No other offering would do, and no other price was too great for His beloved bride.

acg

The Bride Was Born

With just one thrust, sword pierced His side
Birthing God's daughter, His Son's holy Bride.

—ACJ

But one soldier pierced his side with a sword and
immediately blood and water came out.

—John 19:34

The Old Testament was a type of foreshadowing of the
new covenant (Colossians 2:17). We now have a new kingdom beginning with the coming of the second Adam who
is Christ Jesus (2 Corinthians 15:45). The first Adam slept,
signifying a type of death (Genesis 2:21), and through this
death, Eve was created, her blood being produced from the
marrow of Adam's own bone. Oh, how it pleased the triune
God to see Himself so perfectly reflected in these two from
one human being. Just as the first Adam slept, the second
Adam also did, yet in a greater way through actual death.
God's own plan was made perfect. When Jesus cried out, "It
is finished" (John 19:30), His blood was shed for the salvation and redemption of mankind.

This is God's way. Just as the Redeemer came by water
and blood, so has the Redeemed. The moment the sword

penetrated the body of Christ, the hand of God was also moved by the Spirit. With one thrust, He reached in just as He did with first Adam, immediately birthing the daughter of God, the bride of Christ, His eternal partner, His help meet. The seed of God was now deposited in her (1 John 3:9); she became a living being. The first Adam upon seeing his Eve exclaimed,

> Bone of my bone and flesh of my flesh.
> (Genesis 2:23)

The second Adam could now proclaim, after seeing His bride, "Beloved of my Spirit and Blood of my Blood." We are His offspring (Acts 17:28). She didn't awaken immediately though because there still was business that needed to be tended to.

Jesus, our Redeemer, had to plunder hell and loosen the chains of death and the grave (Revelation 1:18). He had to loosen the bands of wickedness and set the captives free (Isaiah 58:6).

> And having spoiled principalities and powers, he made a show of them openly, triumphing over them. (Colossians 2:15)

He preached to those spirits in prison the beautiful redemption story (1 Peter 3:19). It was by His own blood one chain after another fell. Although scripture doesn't name these chains one by one, I can see through the eyes of faith the first chain to be loosened was called racial bias. No longer would ethnicity hold this new daughter back in its chains. Never was this holy bride to hold one race above another (Acts 10:45). Next, with just one drop of his blood, the bands of socioeconomic prejudices were shattered. Never would social status and money dictate her value in God.

Silver and gold have I none. (Acts 3:6)

Finally the chains of gender bias were completely crushed, now no longer an issue "for there is nether Jew nor Greek, bond or free, male or female for we are all one in Christ Jesus (Galatians 3:28). The demons shook and bowed as light conquered darkness. Taking possession of the keys to death and the grave, He led captivity captive (Ephesians 4:8). He has taken it out of the way, having nailed it to the cross.

Fifty days after Passover, coinciding with the customary Hebrew celebration (Leviticus 23:16), the heavenlies were filled with the long-anticipated *Day of Harvest*, the first-fruits of believers. In the upper room gathered 120 followers of Christ awaiting the promise of the "Comforter" (John 15:26). A great sound of a mighty rushing wind filled the room with awesome power (Acts 2:2).

God, now taking a life-giving breath, came forth from deep within His bosom and imparted the life of His Holy Spirit into the nostrils of this young beauty (Acts 2:2–3). On each one appeared a tongue of fire (Acts 2:3) as she uttered her first words crying out, "Abba" (Galatians 4:6), as the Spirit gave her utterance (Acts 2:4).

Reaching her full maturity, she stood dressed in a white robe embodied in the righteousness of the saints (Revelation 19:8). He gazed upon her and saw a diamond brought through the fire of purification. He beheld a reflection of Himself in every facet and said, "This is good!" (Genesis 1:31). Male and female are born into one bride, now completely free to be all He created them to be, having the proof of sonship within (Romans 8:16).

His Burial

And after this Joseph of Arimathaea, being a disciple of
Jesus, but secretly for fear of the Jews, besought Pilate
that he might take away the body of Jesus: and Pilate
gave him leave. He came therefore, and took the body of
Jesus. And there came also Nicodemus, which at the first
came to Jesus by night, and brought a mixture of myrrh
and aloes, about an hundred pound weight. Then took
they the body of Jesus, and wound it in linen clothes
with the spices, as the manner of the Jews to bury.

—John 19:38–40

The gospel of Matthew speaks of Joseph of Arimathaea as
being a rich man, but John adds that he was also a disciple of Jesus. He, being very wealthy, could afford the costly
burial spices of myrrh and aloe used as preservatives in caring
for their dead. He and another disciple named Nicodemus
secretly took the body of Jesus and gently laid Him in Joseph's
new tomb. These men took fine linen and tore it into strips,
soaked them in spices, and wrapped the body using great
detail. It was their custom to wrap each finger, each toe,
arms, legs, and torso individually with many strips of linen
(John 19:40). The entire body was wrapped, excluding His
face. This most delicate duty was to be done by the women
a few days later. The Jewish people believed the spirit stayed

or hovered around the individual for three days and would not embalm their faces until this time had expired. By that time, the wrappings would have solidified, making the body protected and perfectly preserved.

Now on the first day of the week, Mary Magdalene came to complete the process of body preparation as custom dictated. When arriving at the tomb, she observed the stone covering the grave opening had been rolled away.

> Frantic, she immediately ran to Simon Peter and John exclaiming, "They have taken away the Lord out of the sepulchre, and we know not where they have laid Him." (John 20:2)

When the two men arrived at the tomb entrance, John looked in.

Scripture tells us he immediately believed (John 20:8). Peter, then going in, saw the head cloth neatly folded in a place all by itself. This brings two questions to mind. What did John believe? Why was the napkin that had been lying on the Lord's face so puzzling to Peter? Human hands had meticulously taken special time to fold the face cloth and then lay it away from the other grave clothes. (Beloved, any story of one piece of cloth covering the whole body of Jesus is absolutely false, and do not believe it!) Peter possibly recalled the last meal he shared with Jesus and the other disciples. At the end of the meal, Jesus folded His napkin and laid it beside His plate. Reverend Tim McConnell helps us understand the importance of this powerful demonstration: For in those days, the wadded napkin meant "I'm finished." But if the master got up from the table, folded his napkin, and laid it beside his plate, the servant would not dare touch the table, because the folded napkin meant, "I'm coming back!"

(Citizen Times Devotional April 21, 2017). Jesus was foretelling what was to come; He was coming back! What a parallel! John looked in and saw the most marvelous sight one could behold. The grave clothes lying on the stone slab were now perfectly formed to the Savior's body, but John observed only an empty shell! The news of a risen Savior spread like wildfire. With such evidence before them, this news could not be denied. Thousands came to believe as I can picture each of them peering in to see the headcloth folded separately and a perfectly formed shell of a man just crucified days before.

We have to reflect on the religious leaders of that day as well. What could they have been thinking as they watched their world being turned upside down? These men thought that death would be the means to an end for this disruptor, but they quickly found it was only the beginning (Matthew 27:11–15). With many of their priests converting to Christianity (John 12:42), never again would there be business as usual. Although scripture doesn't reveal much about them, upon recovery from shock, they probably began working on a plan to silence this outbreak (Acts 4:18).

No effort on man's part can silence the voice of God whether in a still small voice (1 Kings 19:12) or one out of heaven (Matthew 3:17). His own sheep learn to know and love His voice and follow wherever it may lead them (John 10:27).

Grafting So Complete, Two Become One

The Bridegroom Beckons

Even if I could only bring Him one little grape,
I knew that grape was precious to Him because
I had worked my whole life for it.

—Heidi Baker, *Birthing the Miraculous*

The Lord had come to me in a vision one day. I had been given a rare opportunity to look into what I instinctively knew were the different chambers of my heart. He reached out and took my hand without saying a word as we entered the first chamber. This room was brightly lit, with plush and comfortable furniture making it cozy and inviting. He broke His silence and said, "This is the front room of your heart." I was very pleased as vanity and pride seemed to rise up from nowhere. Then He continued to lead me through another door.

As I stepped over the threshold, I entered a dimly lit room that only received ambient lighting from a broken window in the corner. I could see the glass had been shattered and strewn across the floor. There was no furniture or decor of any kind. The air was chilled, damp, and musty as an old empty farmhouse would be. This place puzzled me greatly since I didn't even know it existed. He broke His silence once more to say, "You never let Me in here, may I come in?" I was utterly astounded! Before I could audibly say yes, but just as fast as I thought it, He was standing in the middle of the room with a broom in His hand. Wow! I knew He had plenty of work to do, but to my surprise, He was absolutely delighted to do it and couldn't wait to get started!

Everyone has areas in their heart that need healing, cleansing, and renewal. For a period in our Christian walk, we can feel relatively comfortable as to how we have changed and developed. The people closest to us may even notice a difference in us, but as we grow, the Holy Bridegroom beckons, saying, "Separate yourself to an even greater degree." This beckoning is His gift to us. It takes God to know God, as the scripture teaches us in that we love Him because He first loved us (1 John 4:19). We begin to receive these holy yearnings by His own choosing.

This is not because we are backslidden but because He's calling for greater intimacy. This is the longing of a born-again believer awakened by the Holy Spirit. The scripture of Song of Solomon 1:2a says,

> Let him kiss me with the kisses of his mouth.

This kiss is an expression of a close, personal relationship, beyond and deeper than our initial love with Him. This was not like the kiss Judas gave Jesus on His cheek, as you would with close friends or family (Matthew 26:49) but the intimacy of the mouth. In this passage of scripture, she asked to "kiss the kisses," the kind of intimacy expressed by constant close fellowship. It is not a natural kissing of the mouth but to kiss the words that proceed from His mouth. These are the kisses she longed for. We must desire to live by every word that proceeds from the mouth of God (Matthew 4:4).

All through scripture, our Holy Bridegroom expresses His love for us. It teaches us that while we were yet sinners,

Christ died for us (Romans 5:8). Right from the beginning, Jesus is seen as the Lamb of God, the One who takes away the sins of the world (John 1:29), crucified before the foundation of the world was ever laid (Revelation 13:8). This is most beautifully illustrated in the parable of the vine.

> I am the vine, ye are the branches. (John 15:1)

Jesus often used parables to teach us. This one in particular wonderfully depicts His nurturing care over our every moment. He has revealed to His own the hidden mysteries through this precious metaphor. *We* are beckoned to abide in Him, to become one with Him just as He is one with His Father (John 17:21).

Looking at the example of the vineyard, we can learn and come to understand the heart of God in a much deeper and clearer way than ever before. The natural branches of this vine can become wild with unruly shoots using up valuable nutrients yet unable to bear fruit. Although pruning is painful, it is necessary for the growth and overall health of the plant. Bearing fruit is the whole purpose of the vine and branch life. The shoots do not develop because they are starved but because of the healthy growth of the previous year. If our ministry has been successful, it is easy for the flesh to get puffed up and rely on its own strength rather than God's. So our success sometimes causes wild shoots to grow, thus necessitating pruning. Year after year, the keeper of the vineyard watches over it, exquisitely demonstrating the care the Father has over us (John 15:1).

> A vineyard of red wine; I, the Lord, do keep it, I will water it every moment; lest

any hurt it, I will keep it night and day.
(Isaiah 27:2)

The triune God is such a glorious unity perfectly at work. God the Father constantly watches over us, God the Son keeps our lives hidden in Him, and God the Holy Spirit is our nourishment.

Just as the grafted branch is connected to the vine receiving its life and nourishment, so is the deepest love God gives and abundantly pours over His children. To make a graft, both the vine and the branch are wounded. Both are brought together by the master of the vineyard, wound to wound, to become one. We see one is an unnatural branch, wounded by sin and death, the other a broken body at Calvary. The very sap that flows in the heavenly vine now fills the daughter branch in perfect conformation concealing where one begins and the other ends.

Scripture teaches us in John 15:4 to abide in Him, and He will abide in us. As our little grafted branch begins to send fibers into the stem of the vine, we partake in a marvelous but mysterious union. The branch can only bear fruit if it has a continuous unbroken relationship with the vine. Yet the vine cannot produce fruit without the branches. A holy dependency develops via the branch's willingness to abide and the vine's willingness to keep it. Abiding is the childlike faith of fixing our eyes on Jesus, our heavenly vine, depending on Him for all. The only way to abide is to spend time with Him, an act of the will! This vital relationship is fed and nurtured by the actual abiding through prayer, fasting, and reading of God's word.

A new life begins. This love relationship, as it says in Song of Songs 1:5a,

Your love is better than wine.

This wine metaphorically refers to the world, and nothing it has to offer can compare to this love. This holy union is by the working of the Holy Spirit, and nothing can substitute. The branch will wither and be fit for the burn pile without the vine. Likewise, to our utter amazement, without the branches, the vine cannot produce the fruit the keeper of the vine is longing to give to those of His choosing.

The story of the fig tree in Mark 11:13–14 has another powerful message for us to glean regarding the bearing of fruit. Jesus was on His way from Bethany when He saw a fig tree alongside the road full of leaves. Scripture clearly also tells us two things about this particular passage. Firstly, it wasn't too early for the harvest of figs, secondly, Jesus was hungry. The tree being in full bloom was a significant factor since figs were produced right alongside the development of its leaves. It was perfectly natural for Jesus to expect an abundance of figs since all the conditions for them were there. Planted in rich soil and ahead of the season, its foliage beckoned the weary to itself. Although beautiful in appearance, this tree had failed in its purpose, a type of hypocrisy by the promise of one thing but giving another. Closeness to the road indicated a purpose of nourishment for weary travelers. Jesus's anger was for lack of fruit, *not* because of hunger. This tree stood tall and beautiful in all its appearance, but just like many of the religious leaders at that time, pious, without power, and blinded by self-beauty, no good to anyone.

I had a vision of a cluster of very large, deep, rich purple grapes, yet one missing from the center. I could see that this one grape had been picked, but I didn't understand the vision until the following week. My next few days were very busy. I led two people to Christ, gave a timely and much-needed prophecy over several hurting people, and gently reprimanded a few who were heading down the wrong path. Added to this was an unusual weight of pressure with regard to my business and family. I suddenly remembered the vision as I felt the Holy Spirit softly whisper, "All on only one grape." Wow! In my immaturity and eagerness, I shouted, "Lord, use me more!"

The Holy Spirit revealed it to be a growing and building process. He wants us to be able to hold up under the crush of the winepress. You see, for every grape He uses, it must be crushed to nourish all those who drink from its fountain. Oswald Chambers explained this beautifully and clearly.

> You cannot be poured-out wine if you remain a whole grape, you cannot be broken bread if you remain whole grain. Grapes have to be crushed, and grain has to be ground, then the sweetness of the life comes out to the glory of God. (*The Complete Works of Oswald Chambers*, p. 674).

A few days later, I again heard the still small voice of the Holy Spirit. This kind of hearing was more of a *knowing*. I realized He was distinctly asking my permission to be used for His redistribution of the fruit to others of His choosing. Did I have a *yes* in my heart? Would I risk it all to serve Him in any way He asked? Although I sensed the rough road that lay ahead, I said yes. It is the choosing of the vine keeper as to whose fruit He uses and its distribution. Ours is to abide and say yes.

Do you have a yes in your heart? It is a yes to prayer and fasting, to bridling your tongue, and to guarding your eyes and ears. When Jesus was in the Garden of Gethsemane, He said yes for us and went into the crucifixion with His eyes wide open. He offered His hands as a living sacrifice and surrendered them to the nails, so our hands may share in the anointing by the blood that flowed from them. He was the first to be crushed and the first to show the way. We have been sanctified, justified, and commissioned through the very life given for us on the cross. He said yes to it all and, because He did, we also can. You see, it was the God of mercy that nailed Him to the cross making Him broken bread and poured out wine. It is the God of mercy watching over our every moment, and it is the God of mercy who forever hides us under the shadow of His wings (Psalm 17:8).

> I've been bought with a price,
> By His blood it is sealed.
> I am resolved to surrender,
> The eternal "yes" is revealed.
> (ACJ)

To All Who Harken,

Please Come In.

The Marriage Supper Will Soon Begin.

The Bridal Relationship and His End-Time Church

*If you knew who God made you to be,
you'd never want to be anyone else.*

—Bill Johnson, Bethel Church, Redding, California

God used the intimacy between husband and wife within the marriage union to represent the relationship between Christ and His church. Although but a shadow, there is nowhere a more fitting description of this blessed mystery. The institution of marriage, the demonstration of two becoming one flesh, has this great and glorious mystery hidden within an everlasting covenant, the church espoused to the one true Husband, Jesus Christ. To love, honor, trust, and obey, oddly; death only brings them closer. She sets herself apart, reserved as a chaste virgin, following her Bridegroom King wherever He leads. He is her tree planted by the rivers of water never to be moved. Leaving all others, she takes absolute delight in the fruit of His tree, eating until satisfied, safe, and protected under His shadow. The analogy of the fleshly marriage can, in part, help us to understand the partnership of this heavenly union.

To understand the consummation process between the church and the Bridegroom, we must first differentiate between the natural and the spiritual body. There are two kinds of bodies: celestial and terrestrial (1 Corinthians 15:40). The celestial is heavenly, and the terrestrial is earthly. Although coexisting, it is important we do not confuse them in our thinking.

> The first Adam was made a living soul:
> the last Adam was made a quickening
> spirit. (1 Corinthians 15:45)

Human beings are made up of flesh and blood that are of earthly material.

When a person dies, the body returns to the dust from whence it came. What we want to stress is the spirit being is made up of material of a *heavenly* substance. This substance is not the flesh and blood as we know it but that of the living God. When we receive Him into our hearts, we are actually receiving His energy, light, nature, and actual Spirit being. Our soul, once dead because of sin, is now alive, born again into this heavenly life. Our body now becomes the recipient of the living God and has the capacity to manifest that rebirth.

Since we know there are no differences in the spirit (Galatians 3:28), we need a clear understanding of the marital relationship between children of God and Christ. It begins with mutual joy freely flowing between Christ and His beloved bride. We are the elect of God, chosen by the One infinitely greater than man or angels:

> I have chosen thee, and not cast thee
> away. (Isaiah 41:9)

From the beginning He was above all men and angels, yet He chose us for His companion. As bridegroom chooses a bride, He chose us to be spirit of His Spirit and blood of His blood above all others (Hebrews 2:16).

> My dove, my undefiled is but one; she is the only one of her mother, she is the choice one of her that bare her. (Song of Solomon 6:9)

> For the Lord hath chosen Zion; he hath desired it for his habitation. (Psalm 132:13)

The stunning reality is that He desired us! It didn't just start with an attraction like most love relationships. His love for us was, and is, and is to come, a burning desire, for a forever flame. We are His beloved from eternity past, present, and future. Our love toward Him is weak in the beginning, but as we come to Him, our weak love begins to mature. The consummation with Christ and His bride begins here with hearts in full agreement with His. This agreement is ushered in by our extravagant worship as the bride becomes lovesick over her Betrothed. He declares,

> Thou art beautiful, O my love. (Song of Solomon 6:4)

History teaches that at one time the city of Tirzah was the most beautiful of all Gentile nations. This is a comparison of the beauty of believers in a perverse world. As the entire body of Christ begins to engage in this extravagant worship, the fragrance of Christ emanates. The Holy Spirit is bringing together this intimate partnership that facilitates for proliferates, our place in the heart of the Bridegroom King. We are transformed as we become a blazing fire, reflecting His eyes of fire (Revelation 19:12). He has chosen His beloved church above all others. Just as He has chosen her, above all else, she has also chosen Him. Rejecting all other suitors for His sake, having the one and only desire to please Him, the sought-after pearl of great price (Matthew 13:46). In ancient Israel, the firstfruits of the harvest always belonged to God. We are His inheritance, the firstfruit to God and the Lamb (Revelation 14:4). Of His will, He begat us to be the first-fruits of His peculiar ones (James 1:18).

As we gaze into His eyes of fire, He reflects back into ours the most tender and ardent love. Oh, that we might know in our inner man the width and length and depth and height the love of Christ which passes all knowledge (Ephesians 3:18–19). His love for us valiantly proved stronger than death. He bids us to come to eat at His table. "Eat, Oh friends, drink, Yea drink abundantly, Oh beloved" (Song of Solomon 5:1b), in unending fellowship. Mutual rejoicing and communion are joint participation for the heart of the good for each other. It is not a one-sided dining, as He is with us also. The bride says,

> Let my Beloved come into his garden and eat his pleasant fruit. (Song of Solomon 4:16)

His answer to her is as follows:

> I am come into my garden, my sister, my spouse; I have gathered my myrrh with my spice, I have honeycomb with my honey, I have drunk my wine with my milk. (Song of Solomon 5:1a)

We are betrothed to Him through our conversion. The time is coming when we will enter His house.

> With gladness and rejoicing they shall be brought; they shall enter into the king's palace. (Psalm 45:15)

We shall join Him at His banquet table eternally enjoying His embraces.

This is the intimacy of the bridal paradigm and reflection of the end-time church. The believers clothe themselves in this reality, which ultimately gives them the power to win the lost for the kingdom.

The Water of Life

*Oh God, I have tasted Thy goodness, and it has both
satisfied me and made me thirsty for more.*

—A. W. Tozar

And the Spirit and the Bride say, "come," and let him
who hears say "come," and let them who thirst come.
Whoever desires, let him take of the waters of life.

—Revelation 22:17

The Spirit and the bride work in perfect unity. The
Bridegroom King loves the sound of His Beloved's voice.
It is time we take our privileged position and stand as His
warriors in worship (Matthew 11:12), intercession, and
especially as His beloved bride. This bridal relationship
means we have intimate knowledge of the loving heart of
God. This bridal paradigm is not a gender issue. It is where
pure male power and absolute female gentleness embrace
and become the bride. King David's desire was to "behold
the beauty of the Lord" (Psalm 27:4). He was a man after
God's own heart (Acts 13:22). He learned to see God with
the eyes of his heart, regardless of what was raging around
him.

For a long time, I could not focus my heart on worship. My thoughts wandered constantly on everything but Jesus. One day, out of sheer frustration with myself, I laid my head down on the kitchen table using the back of my hands as a type of pillow and cried out, "Why am I so weak?" "How long will You be patient with me?" In that moment, as my forehead pressed gently against my fingers, and as I recognized the darkness of my own soul, revelation came flooding in so clearly. I saw the feet of Jesus not only in a vision but also through the pressure of my forehead against my fingers; it was like resting on His feet. I immediately became intimately connected to my Savior. I could envision the nail prints on His feet and began to thank Him for all He had done for me. The tears of sorrow became tears of joy. The anointed visitation of that morning still continues every time I meet Him in faith, intimate worship with a true and living God. This is the bridal relationship we must long for.

Every religion claims to hold the only truth, the only way, but their gods do not have eyes to see or ears to hear. They are distant and cold, without mercy, without heart, and unable to sympathize with our weaknesses because they have no life in them. When *we* worship, we get in touch with the inner source of *our* living indwelling God (Acts 2:4), who has taken up residency inside us. We become the temple of the Holy Spirit (2 Corinthians 6:16), what an awesome privilege!

I had a vision of a large glass pitcher. It was bubbling over with crystal-clear water and seemingly an endless stream gushing with great force. As the pitcher poured, it filled three glasses, which in turn gushed just like the pitcher. I noticed a hole in the base of the pitcher about the size of a quarter. This was where the flood of water was coming from. Not from the top as with a normal filling, but from beneath, the bottom of the pitcher. It was a wonderful picture of a life connected with the true Source. Scripture says,

> Out of our bellies will flow rivers of Living Water. (John 7:38)

It affects all those around us. The pitcher was not only filled but became demonstrative of God's overflowing power to point the way and fill others as well.

In ancient Israel, the Jewish High Priest would perform sacrifices in the temple. In this temple was an outer court and an inner chamber separated by a veil. This inner chamber was called the Holy of Holies, a place where the Spirit of God dwelled here on earth. The area beyond the veil was forbidden to all except the High Priest placing the sacrificial blood on the mercy seat for Himself and all the people once a year (Leviticus 16:15). The temple veil tore in half from top to bottom the minute Jesus died on the cross (Mark 15:38). This represented the crucified flesh of Christ being torn in two for us, making a way for us to go directly into the Holy of holies (Hebrews 10:20).

Rather than sacrificing year after year as was the Jewish tradition, our High Priest, Jesus Christ (Hebrews 5:10), not only shed His holy blood but also poured it over the altar of the mercy seat Himself. This sacrifice was perfect (Hebrews 10:12) and never needed to be repeated since His blood perpetually flows (Hebrews 10:10). Past the outer court of our hearts deep within the inner chamber is where the Holy Spirit resides in a believer:

> Know ye not ye are the temple of the Holy Spirit? (1 Corinthians 6:19)

His holy and perfect blood is sprinkled on the altar of our hearts and carried around in earthen vessels. It is the only blood that satisfies the heart of God for the forgiveness of sins.

Beyond this veil are what scripture records as the very presence of God. How do we connect with this True Source? What is the secret to having our lives gush with the river of living water? There is only one path, beloved; and that is through prayer, fasting, and the word of God. I don't mean the kind of prayer where you're only asking God for things but where your whole heart is engaged in supplication, worship, and fasting, the life of a true worshipper.

> O, let the place of secret prayer become
> to me the most beloved spot on earth.
> (Andrew Murray)

The Oil of Intimacy

God releases more of His power and presence
according to the measure of our hunger for Him.

—anonymous

Jesus told a parable likening the kingdom of heaven to ten virgins going out to meet the Bridegroom (Matthew 25:1). He used this analogy as revelation depicting Himself, the Bridegroom King, and the church, His bride. Upon studying this story, it is an awakening reality to know that in the end days, only half were truly ready when the Bridegroom came to receive them unto Himself. It is noteworthy to see all the virgins in this story were asleep. They all had to be awakened at the hour of the Bridegroom's arrival. This isn't a type of spiritual sleep as half were ready at a moment's notice to get up and go when beckoned. This truly represents their every-day living; we see that all were about their daily lives. It also represents this side of heaven, His bride in her earthen vessel. The lamps are each individual's personal ministry. The oil is the intimacy of a secret life of prayer.

Above all ministries, jobs, or business opportunities, our priority must be to pursue the oil of intimacy; no one can give this to us (Matthew 25:7–9). It can only be acquired by spending time in loving fellowship with God. We are sons of

God by Christ Jesus and the bride of Christ through redemption, awaiting our Bridegroom King.

Do not confuse a growing church or ministry for the anointing of the Holy Spirit. Our ministries can be booming with growth and still be without the oil of intimacy. The five foolish virgins missed the opportunity to be used by the manifest presence of the Holy Spirit because they did not cultivate the oil of intimacy with a living God. They were busy doing the things of their own ministries yet not taking time to personally connect with God. We know they each had the born-again experience because they all had lamps (salvation) and were referred to as virgins (sons of God), but they lacked the oil of intimacy, dried up, and were without their first love. Without having the oil, it is impossible to have the anointing of a bridal walk. By the time these five foolish ones came to realize the Bridegroom was on His way, there simply wasn't enough time to fill their lamps. This kind of intimacy must grow individually over a period of time. The end-time wave of revival is coming, and if we want to be active, anointed servants of God, we must take the time now to fill our lamps.

We are told to watch and pray (Mark 14:38) without ceasing (1 Thessalonians 5:17). Our instructions are to pray for laborers in the harvest, the peace of Jerusalem, and many other areas of our lives. We are to speak to ourselves in psalms and spiritual songs and be intimately connected to our Savior in prayer, supplication, and especially worship. We are to follow Jesus who is making intercession for us daily before the throne of grace. If we connect with Him on this level of intercessory prayer, we can change the world around us, literally wresting some out of the fire (Jude 23).

Many around us do not realize the late hour we are in. Our Bridegroom King will be coming soon, searching out those whose lamps are full and ready to hear the midnight cry to go and meet Him (Matthew 25:13). If we are not spending time cultivating an intimate prayer life, then we better hasten with it before time runs out. Our main goal, even above our ministry, is to actively pursue the oil of intimacy, without it, there is no anointing. The Spirit and the bride find unity, in this place of intimacy (Revelation 22:17). If we desire involvement in the next wave of revival as useful workers in the harvest, we must be counted among the wise.

As we draw nearer to the Lord, our hearts are tenderized. We become lovesick for Him (Song of Songs 2:5). The Bridegroom Himself reveals His ravished heart over us, even with the weakest and smallest of glances His way (Song of Songs 4:9–10). As a Bridegroom rejoices over his bride, our God rejoices over us (Isaiah 62:4–7). God calls us to this higher bridal identity as the Holy Spirit raises up forerunners to prepare His church for her greatest hour.

> Behold I come quickly and my reward is
> with me. (Revelation 22:12)

The following page demonstrates *our spiritual journey* and the kind of activities that make up a believer's life of devotion. To be filled with the oil of intimacy, we must be active in the pursuit of God.

Ye Are The Salt Of The Earth

ac Jr

The Divine Union

A wedding is an event, but a marriage is a life.

—Dr. Myles Monroe

The bride of Christ has adorned herself in the wedding garment (Revelation 19:7, 8) and made ready for the blessed union with her beloved Bridegroom King. In Song of Songs, chapter 1, verse 4, we hear the bride say,

> The king hath brought me into his chambers.

She realized all was freely given to her (Romans 5:5). All His personal possessions, His wealth, His peace, and joy were lavishly poured out upon her.

> Blessed are they which are called to the marriage supper of the Lamb. (Revelation 19:9)

To this end, the Savior poured out His soul whose primary mission was rescue of His Beloved from the grips of death. This long-awaited day will neither happen because of a great army nor be accomplished with corruptible things such as silver or gold. This can be done exclusively by the blood of our Warrior Lamb.

This union came at an enormous cost to the bride. She had suffered greatly at the hands of ruthless, godless, and perverse generations. She was tortured, thrown into prison, beaten, abandoned, persecuted, and beheaded (Revelation 20:4) yet never forgotten. Her beauty, grace, and strength flourished (Romans 8:28) in the depths of the furnace of affliction. All throughout this earthly wilderness, she continually leaned upon her Beloved (Song of Solomon 8:5). Although she was a stranger and a pilgrim in search of that promised city (1 Peter 2:11), His constant wooing caused her lovesick heart (Song of Solomon 2:5) to press on. He set Himself as a seal upon her heart (Song of Solomon 8:6), branding her every thought and action with the perfect image of Himself.

In the beginning, God spoke all heaven and its contents into existence but *not* mankind. He carefully crafted and formed *us* with His own hands, fully investing Himself. In the male was instilled His power and strength, and in the female, His beauty and tenderness. Since the first Adam and his beloved bride were earthly, their consummation was set within the boundaries established by God Himself, in Genesis chapter 1. As in the earthly union, God in His infinite wisdom passionately imparted His own attributes to create a beautiful bride for the second Adam, His beloved Son. This *one bride* is in the full power and strength of man and the full beauty and tenderness of woman, both critical to stand complete in Christ and in maturity, as one body (Philippians 3:21). Perfectly conformed to His Son, the bride has been prepared for the heavenly marriage. Unlike earthly marriage, heavenly marriage is that of the spirit, one with Christ, one mind, one desire, and most importantly, one heart.

We will have resurrected bodies that had been sown in corruption but raised incorruptibly (1 Corinthians 15:53), a real body that can eat and drink but not suffer. When Jesus spoke with the apostles after the resurrection, they did not recognize Him (John 21:4), until He showed His nail-scarred palms. The bride is washed in the blood of the Lamb, dressed in pure white, radiant in righteousness, and never again to see decay. All heaven awaits this glorious day.

This eternal union will now reign with one emotion, intellect, and will, while dwelling in a new heaven and earth (Revelation 21:1–2). The old will pass away by fire (2 Peter 3:12–13), ushering in the end of time and the beginning of eternity.

God's desire is to be with us. The New Jerusalem is the place where God dwells with His own, Jew and Gentile alike, face to face with the one true and living God, ruling and reigning with Him. He will have made us kings and priests to rule and reign with Him forever (Revelation 1:6).

Come To The Table

acg

In the Prayer Closet

Christ gave us his flesh for food, his blood for drink, his soul as our price, the water from his side for our cleansing.

—Bernard of Clairvaux in 1665

Jesus the same yesterday, and today and forever.

—Hebrews 13:8

I could not close without first taking time to discuss the importance of a personal prayer life/time. Although this can look and be as different as we are individuals, observing others can help us as well. If I were to say I have an intimate relationship with my husband but never spend time with him, how could I honestly say we were close or even knew each other very well? However, we consider, confide, and converse in nearly every decision we make.

Our Savior deserves nothing less, preferably more.

I dreamed one night I saw a man sitting in a restaurant being served one dish after another not fit to be eaten. As each dish came before him, he stated, "Add more salt!"

I thought to myself, *How can salt do anything to help?* When I awakened, I listened to a YouTube message by Dutch Sheets on "Give Him 15" (March 23, 2022) regarding *salt*. Was this coincidence or the plan of God for me that morning?

Ye are the salt of the earth. (Matthew
5:13–16)

Let your speech be always with grace sea-
soned with salt. (Colossians 4:6)

Salt is used to preserve, season, and enhance many
things even in our own natural body. A balance (homeostasis) is needed to maintain healthy kidneys, heart, and liver
functions as well. In our walk with Christ, we must maintain
spiritual homeostasis through a relationship of intimacy.

But if the salt have lost its savour, where-
with shall it be salted? It is thenceforth
good for nothing. (Matthew 5:13)

Sheet's post that morning solidified exactly what God
wanted from me and from us. In our everyday walk, we are
to be the salt that seasons everything our lives touch, remem-
bering that through us, He renews and restores all. We are
to be a positive people, holy and peculiarly in love with our
Savior while reaching out to a desperate world. This begins
in our prayer closet.

In 1 Corinthians 11:23–34, Paul teaches his listeners
that he received revelation from the Holy Spirit about the
Lord's supper (communion meal). He was not present personally when Jesus taught His disciples; however, the text
here in 1 Corinthians has become our primary source. God
chooses to come to us through ways we can understand.
Bread is something we know and need to sustain our lives.

Jesus said, "I AM the bread of life." (John
6:35)

We can come to know this *bread* both physically and spiritually through holy participation in the communion meal. God's desire is to fellowship with us as Adam and Eve being the first witness of this truth in the garden. God expresses His desire to be one with us and explained it this way:

> In the beginning was the Word, and the Word was with God, and the Word was God. (John 1:1)

> And the Word became flesh, and dwelt among us. (John 1:14)

The culmination of this *oneness* is expressed so beautifully in the communion meal.

The early church leaders taught, "The Son of God became the Son of Man so that the sons of men might become sons of God." This is astounding when we consider God wanted to be with us so much that no price was too great. It is breathtaking to think the God of the universe humbled Himself and made a way to have intimate fellowship with us through His love. He made a way where there was no way.

> On the night Jesus was betrayed, "Jesus took bread and blessed it, and brake it, and gave it to the disciples, and said, Take, eat; this is my body. And he took the cup, and gave thanks, and gave it to them, saying, Drink ye all of it; For this is my blood of the new testament, which is shed for many for the remission of sins." (Matthew 26:20–29)

Through these scriptures, we learn that bread and wine become His body and blood. Apostle Paul gives further revelation of the communion meal, saying,

> This do ye oft as ye drink it, in remembrance of me. (1 Corinthians 11:24–25)

We can become *one* with Him; consume Him through the communion meal, and in doing so, He consumes and becomes *one* with us.

The Communion Meal

Prepare a small piece of bread and about one to two ounces of drink (wine or juice).

Step 1

This is the most intimate and holy time of your daily devotion. Our attitude must be reverent, and sincere. At the onset, we begin by searching our own hearts for sin through self-examination. Take a deep breath, and as you slowly exhale, feel yourself sink down bowing low in gratitude and humility before God. Ask the Holy Spirit to reveal any sinful areas in your life. Apostle Paul warns that unworthy participation can lead to sickness, weakness, and even death (1 Corinthians 11:30). Having said that however, remember the cross was for sinners—*all of us*—so do not allow weaknesses to keep you away. When we repent, He is faithful to forgive, and better yet, He forgets! To make forgiveness very clear, it's the blood of Christ that completely satisfies the heart of God. During this holy time of prayer in your heart, cover yourself with the blood of Christ. We can come boldly into His presence knowing the blood redeems us—it never changes! Now we can confidently draw near (Hebrews 10:19, 22) because the blood of Jesus satisfies the requirements of God and the cross brings complete deliverance. Watchman Nee once said,

"The blood deals with the sins, and the cross deals with the sinner." How true.

Step 2

Apostle Paul stated,

> For as often as ye eat this bread, and drink this cup, ye shew the Lord's death till he comes. (1 Corinthians 11:26)

Why would this be so important to the early Christians and relevant to us today? Through the communion meal, we have a tangible sign, one we hold in our hands, see with our eyes, taste with our mouths, and physically apply to our hearts. When we enter into this perfect union, know Christ is there.

Lift up the communion elements and bless them. Exclaim the Lord's suffering on the cross, death, and resurrection. You are proclaiming to all of heaven, even extending outward to the principalities and powers of darkness that you believe in Jesus Christ, His body, His blood, and His resurrection power, and the true Lamb of God who gave Himself for us.

Visualize the stripes on His back and emphatically state you believe in all the healing they afford. When we remember His sacrifice, death, and resurrection, we are identifying ourselves with it. This very act pulls into our lives His very presence and power of His resurrected life. At this time, bring in your loved ones claiming all the blessings the cross promises. By faith, place their infirmities in His stripes and declare healing in His holy name. In obedience, when we partake in the communion meal, a spiritual transaction invites the manifestation of the Holy Spirit in our lives. This blessed sacrament brings in health, and wholeness, and even renews youthfulness.

> But they that wait upon the Lord shall renew their strength; they shall mount up with wings as eagles, they shall run and not be weary, they shall walk, and not faint. (Isaiah 40:31)

Remember, as we consume the bread, He was crushed for us. He became broken bread and poured out wine on the altar of the cross. When drinking the cup by faith, picture it permeating every part of your being.

> For the life of the flesh is in the blood and I have given it to you upon the altar to make atonement for your souls; for it is the blood that maketh an atonement for the soul. (Leviticus 17:11)

As we discussed in a prior chapter, our own natural blood has amazing healing power, how much more in His holy blood?

Abide in me, and I in you. (John 15:4)

Believe He is restoring your strength and renewing your mind. Finally, thank Him for giving us a way to tangibly connect with Him. Our lives are being transformed into His image with each transaction we engage in during the communion meal.

Finally

With deep gratitude, thank Him for His presence and for the communion meal where we are sweetly connected by His Holy Spirit. Until the day we stand face to face, it's time to enjoy fellowship and intimacy where *oneness* begins to take its place.

I have come to know personally this act of worship pleases God. I have made this holy sacrament a regular part of my devotion in prayer each morning. The intimacy is immeasurable, and the revelation I receive throughout the day is absolutely undeniable. I love how Jentezen Franklin framed it:

> Communion is a "Your House" experience,
> not just a "Church House" experience.

I'm sure you have heard of or have witnessed couples who have been together so long they begin to look alike. It is natural to pick up mannerisms, expressions, and even the appearance of those you are intimately involved with on a regular basis. If this is true of our natural relationship (it is worth repeating), how much more in the spiritual? No truer statement has been said: "You are the company you keep."

Note to Ponder

God with and among us did not end at the cross. On the contrary, it became the path to make us His own. Incredibly, the God of the universe humbled Himself by becoming a man, endured the cross, conquered death, and rose again all for love. We are one with Him when obedient to observe and participate in the communion meal. For this reason, we can say, when we consume Him, He consumes us.

Song by S. L. Stone (1866)

The Church's one foundation
Is Jesus Christ, her Lord;
She is His new creation
By water and the Word.
From heav'n He came and sought her
To be His holy bride;
With His own blood He bought her,
And for her life He died.

Elect from ev'ry nation,
Yet one o'er all the earth;
Her charter of salvation:
One Lord, one faith, one birth.
One holy name she blesses,
Partakes one holy food,
And to one hope she presses
With ev'ry grace endued.

Through toil and tribulation
And tumult of her war
She waits the consummation
Of peace forevermore
Till with the vision glorious
Her longing eyes are blest,
And the great Church victorious
Shall be the Church at rest.

Yet she on earth has union
With God, the Three in One,
And mystic sweet communion
With those whose rest is won.
O blessed heav'nly chorus!
Lord, save us by Your grace That we, like saints before us,
May see You face to face.

Our Spiritual Journey and Scripture References

Your capacity to receive is based on your hunger to pursue.

—anonymous

A. *First commandment, first place*

And thou shalt love the Lord thy God with all thy heart, and with all thy soul, and with all thy mind, and with all thy strength: this is the first commandment. (Mark 12:30)

B. *Love thy neighbor as thyself*

And second is like, namely this, thou shalt love thy neighbor as thyself. There is none other command greater than these. (Mark 12:31)

C. *Intercession*

And He cometh, and findeth them sleeping, and saith unto Peter, "Simon, sleepest thou? Couldest not thou watch one hour?" (Mark 14:37)

In everything by prayer and supplication with thanksgiving let your requests be made known unto God. (Philippians 4:6)

D. *Worship, praise, family, friends, country, Israel, those in leadership/authority*

By Him therefore let us offer the sacrifice of praise to God continually, that is, the fruit of our lips giving thanks to His name. (Hebrews 13:15)

E. *Study/meditate*

Study to show thyself approved unto God, a workman that needeth not to be ashamed, rightly dividing the word of truth. (2 Timothy 2:15)

F. *Thanksgiving*

O give thanks unto the Lord; for He is good: for His mercy endureth forever. (Psalm 136:1)

G. *Tithe*

Bring ye all the tithes into the storehouse, that there may be meat in mine house, and prove me now herewith, saith the

Lord of hosts, if I will not open you the windows of heaven, and pour you out a blessing, that there shall not be room enough to receive it. (Malachi 3:10)

H. *Fellowship*

Not forsaking the assembling of yourselves together, as the manner of some is; but exhorting one another: so much the more, as ye see the day approaching. (Hebrews 10:25)

I. *Positive-thought life*

Finally, brethren, whatsoever things are true, whatsoever things are honest, whatsoever things are just, whatsoever things are pure, whatsoever things are lovely, whatsoever things are of good report; if there be any virtue, and if there be any praise, think on these things. (Philippians 4:8)

J. *Fasting often*

But the days will come when the Bridegroom shall be taken away from them, and then shall they fast in those days. (Luke 5:35)

K. *Good works*

Yea, a man may say, thou hast faith, and I have works: show me thy faith without thy works, and I will show thee my faith by my works. (James 2:18)

L. *Missions*

And He said unto then, go ye into all the world, and preach the gospel to every creature. (Mark 16:15–16)

M. *Ministry*

And he gave some apostles, and some, prophets; and some, evangelists; and some, pastors and teachers; for the perfecting of the saints, for the work of the ministry, for the edifying of the body of Christ. (Ephesians 4:11–12)

N. *Testify*

O give thanks unto the Lord; call upon his name; make known his deeds among the people. (Psalm 105:1)

The main message of this chapter is this: You will never know someone intimately if you don't spend time together.

I Give You My Heart

The death of Jesus was the opening and the emptying of the full heart of God; it was the out-gushing of that ocean of infinite mercy that heaved and panted and longed for an outlet; It was God showing how he could love a poor guilty sinner.

—Octavius Winslow

Scripture clearly teaches us that all our righteousness is as filthy rags (Isaiah 64:6). If we want to receive salvation, we can never do it on our own merit. We cannot be carried in through natural birth; therefore, parental convictions do not cover us. We must recognize our own need for a Savior and know there is only one way (John 14:6) to attain the kingdom of heaven. Any other way is the same as being a thief and a robber (John 10:1). Beloved, it will not work.

We need to ask Him to forgive us for our sins, for He alone is faithful and just to forgive us and wash us clean from all unrighteousness (1 John 1:9). Through this simple prayer, we are promised if we would give Jesus our hearts, He would come in and dine with us (Revelation 3:20). Open your heart now and talk to Him as you would a trusted friend.

> Lord Jesus, You stand at the door of my
> heart and knock. I ask You to forgive me
> for my sins. I invite You to come and live

inside my heart. By faith, I receive the free gift of eternal life that can only come through You. By faith, I am now born again into the family of God. Thank You for filling me with Your Holy Spirit as I stand a new creation in Christ. Amen.

I encourage you to reach out and tell someone of this life-changing step you've just taken.

The Lord bless thee, and keep thee; The Lord make his face shine upon thee, and be gracious unto thee; The Lord lift up his countenance upon thee, and give thee peace. (Numbers 6:24–26)

Lord Jesus Christ, We Humbly Pray

Song by Henry Eyster Jacobs (1844–1932)

Lord Jesus Christ, we humbly pray
That we may feast on You today;
Beneath these forms of bread and wine
Enrich us with Your grace divine.

Give us, who share this wondrous food,
Your body broken and Your blood,
The grateful peace of sins forgiv'n,
The certain joys of heirs of heav'n.

By faith Your Word has made us bold
To seize the gift of love retold;
All that You are we here receive,
And all we are to You we give.

One bread, one cup, one body, we,
Rejoicing in our unity,
Proclaim Your love until You come
To bring Your scattered loved ones home.

Lord Jesus Christ, we humbly pray,
Oh, keep us steadfast till that day
When each will be Your welcomed guest
In heaven's high and holy feast.

About the Author

Alice Claire Johnson was born in Pontiac, Michigan, on August 11, 1955. She is the middle child of eleven. She earned her degree as a registered nurse, specializing in gerontology (care for the elderly). Her journey to seek a greater understanding of the holy relationship between Jesus and His church has led to this second edition. You will learn, as she did, Jesus never gave up His deity coming to earth and dying on the cross. You will be astounded to discover the power of His blood and how parallel it is to ours. It is her hope that upon reading, you will also grow deeper in love with our Savior. She believes a devoted heart to God and determination to succeed can overcome any obstacles. She is an ordinary woman who loves to tell an extraordinary story.

Printed in the USA
CPSIA information can be obtained
at www.ICGtesting.com
CBHW030814100524
8227CB00008B/55